INVESTIGATE!

MYSTERIES OF SPACE

CAN HUMANS LIVE ON OTHER PLANETS?

BY DONNA REYNOLDS

Enslow PUBLISHING

Please visit our website, www.enslow.com.
For a free color catalog of all our high-quality books, call toll free 1-800-398-2504 or fax 1-877-980-4454.

Cataloging-in-Publication Data

Names: Reynolds, Donna.
Title: Can humans live on other planets? / Donna Reynolds.
Description: New York : Enslow Publishing, 2024. | Series: Mysteries of space | Includes glossary and index.
Identifiers: ISBN 9781978535213 (pbk.) | ISBN 9781978535220 (library bound) | ISBN 9781978535237 (ebook)
Subjects: LCSH: Habitable planets–Juvenile literature. | Space colonies–Juvenile literature. | Space environment–Juvenile literature.
Classification: LCC QB820.R69 2024 | DDC 523.2'4 -dc23

Portions of this work were originally authored by Michael Portman and published as *Could We Live on Other Planets?* All new material this edition authored by Donna Reynolds.

Published in 2024 by
Enslow Publishing
2544 Clinton Street
Buffalo, NY 14224

Designer: Tanya Dellaccio Keeney
Editor: Jennifer Lombardo

Photo credits: Cover (logo) AAVAA/Shutterstock.com; series background Molibdenis/Shutterstock.com; cover Gorodenkoff/Shutterstock.com; p. 5 (right) Sahara Prince/Shutterstock.com; p. 5 (left) Apostle/Shutterstock.com; p. 7 Pearl-diver/Shutterstock.com; p. 8 buradaki/Shutterstock.com; p. 9 Honourr/Shutterstock.com; p. 11 Kira001/Shutterstock.com; pp. 13 (both), 23 (top) courtesy of NASA; p. 15 NASA/JPL-Caltech/MSSS; p. 17 Rob Bayer/Shutterstock.com; p. 19 (top) mkarco/Shutterstock.com; p. 19 (bottom) Rick_Jo/Shutterstock.com; p. 21 Pauline Mongarny/Shutterstock.com; p. 23 (bottom) Kent Weakley/Shutterstock.com; p. 25 (top) Tatiana Grozetskaya/Shutterstock.com; p. 27 Brita Seifert/Shutterstock.com; p. 29 NASA/Ames/JPL-Caltech.

Printed in the United States of America

CPSIA compliance information: Batch #CSENS24: For further information contact Enslow Publishing at 1-800-398-2504.

CONTENTS

Words in the glossary appear in **bold** type the first time they are used in the text.

THE PERFECT PLACE

There are billions of planets in the **universe**, but Earth is the only one we know of that holds life. This is because Earth has certain things no other known planet has. One important thing it has is liquid water. If the planet were closer to the sun, the water would boil away; if it were farther away, the water would freeze.

Scientists call this sweet spot the "Goldilocks zone" or the "habitable zone." Any other planets humans might want to live on would have to be in the habitable zone.

THE HABITABLE ZONE IS FARTHER AWAY FROM A STAR THAT GIVES OFF A LOT OF HEAT, LIKE THE ONE ON THE LEFT. THE HABITABLE ZONE IS CLOSER TO A STAR THAT'S COOLER, LIKE THE ONE ON THE RIGHT.

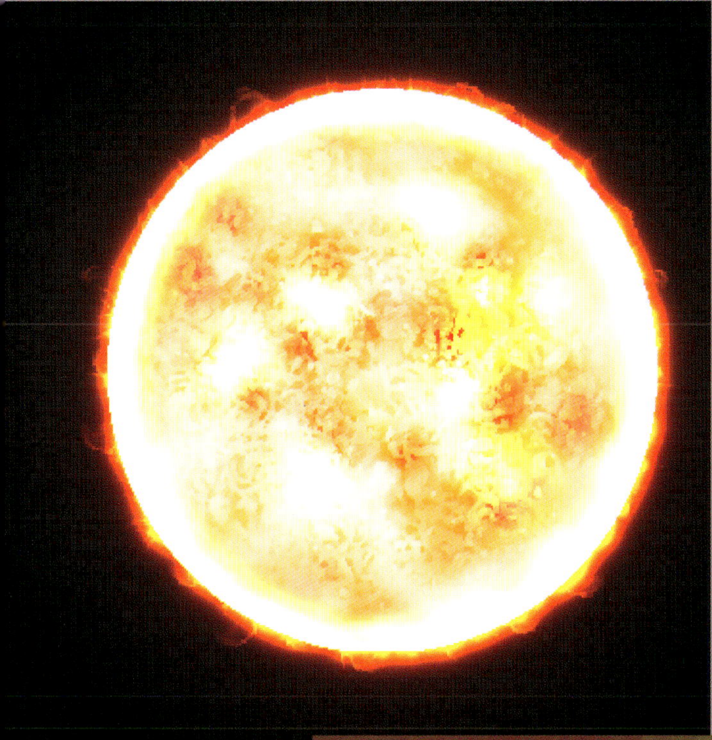

EXPLORE MORE!

HABITABLE MEANS ABLE TO BE LIVED IN. THE HABITABLE ZONE IS DIFFERENT FOR EACH **SOLAR SYSTEM**. IT DEPENDS ON HOW BRIGHT THE SOLAR SYSTEM'S STAR IS, HOW BIG EACH PLANET AROUND IT IS, AND MANY OTHER THINGS.

AN IMPORTANT LIQUID

All life on Earth needs water to survive, or stay alive. Some plants and animals can go without it for long periods of time, but they still need it. Humans need water every day to stay healthy.

Scientists think there might be planets out there where life doesn't need water. However, humans could never live on those planets. Not only would we not have anything to drink, we wouldn't be able to grow any food. We also wouldn't be able to clean ourselves!

A CAMEL CAN LIVE UP TO 15 DAYS WITHOUT WATER. A HUMAN CAN ONLY SURVIVE FOR ABOUT THREE DAYS WITHOUT IT.

EXPLORE MORE!

TOO MUCH WATER ON A PLANET WOULD ALSO BE BAD FOR HUMANS! WE WOULDN'T BE ABLE TO LIVE ON ANY PLANET THAT WAS COVERED COMPLETELY IN WATER WITHOUT SPECIAL TOOLS, BUILDINGS, AND MORE.

A SAFE ATMOSPHERE

Another thing that's important for life is Earth's **atmosphere**. The atmosphere keeps the sun's heat in. Without it, Earth would look like Mars—rocky, dry, and cold. Our atmosphere is also what allows us to breathe. If people want to live on the surface of another planet without always wearing spacesuits, the planet must have an atmosphere very similar to Earth's.

The atmosphere has a third job: keeping us safe from the sun's harmful **radiation**. On any planet that can't keep this radiation out, humans would quickly get sick and die.

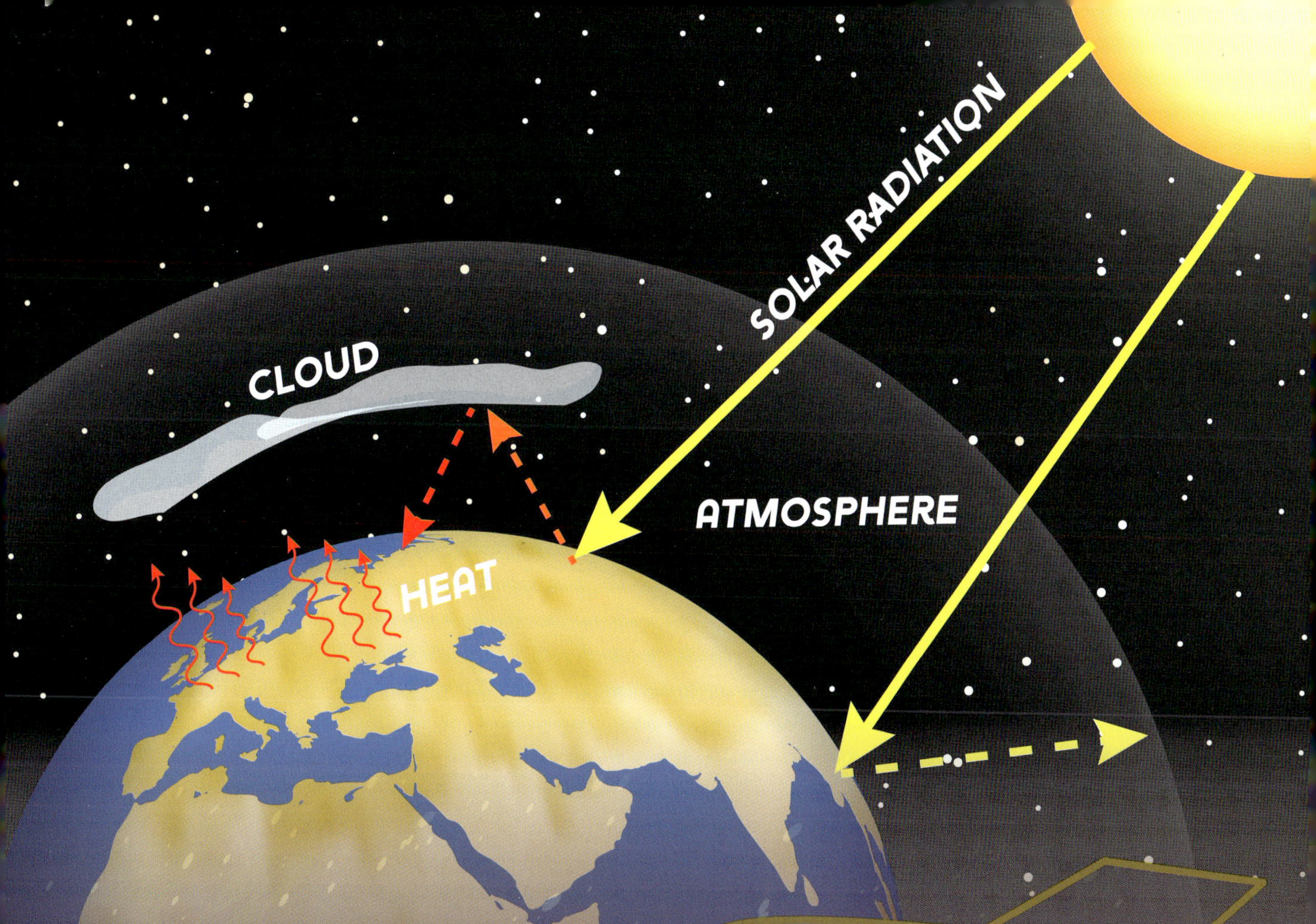

EARTH'S ATMOSPHERE DOESN'T HOLD ALL OF THE SUN'S HEAT. IF IT DID, WE'D BE COOKED! SOME OF IT BOUNCES BACK INTO SPACE.

EXPLORE MORE!

EARTH'S ATMOSPHERE PUSHES DOWN ON THE PLANET, CREATING **PRESSURE**. WITHOUT THIS PRESSURE, WE WOULDN'T HAVE WEATHER.

JUST RIGHT

The **temperature** of a planet plays a big part in deciding what can survive on that planet. On Earth, some creatures can survive in very hot or very cold places. For example, a polar bear is comfortable in the snow, but a person without the right clothing on would freeze.

On another planet, the temperature would need to be within a certain range for humans to survive. However, we have to think about comfort as well as survival. You might be able to live on a planet that's always 120°F (49°C), but would you want to?

EXPLORE MORE!

HUMIDITY IS A MEASURE OF HOW MUCH WATER IS IN THE AIR. PEOPLE GENERALLY FEEL MORE COMFORTABLE WITH HIGHER TEMPERATURES IN PLACES WHERE THE HUMIDITY IS LOW.

A PLANET COVERED IN ICE WOULD BE NEARLY IMPOSSIBLE FOR HUMANS TO LIVE ON FOR MORE THAN A FEW DAYS.

STAYING FIT

When people think of astronauts, they often think of living without **gravity**. However, because humans **evolved** on a planet with gravity, it plays a big part in keeping our bodies healthy. On a smaller planet with less gravity, we would weigh less and our **muscles** would shrink and weaken.

On the other hand, if a planet were bigger than Earth, its gravity would be stronger and we might have a hard time moving around. We would likely also have problems with our **joints** as the weight pressed down on them constantly over time.

EXPLORE MORE!

AS PEOPLE AGE, THEY OFTEN HAVE PROBLEMS WITH THEIR KNEES. THIS IS BECAUSE THE KNEES HAVE TO SUPPORT ALL OF OUR WEIGHT MOST OF THE TIME. ON A PLANET WITH HIGHER GRAVITY, EVEN YOUNG PEOPLE WOULD LIKELY HAVE KNEE PAIN.

ASTRONAUTS ON THE INTERNATIONAL SPACE STATION (ISS) MUST EXERCISE FOR AT LEAST TWO HOURS EVERY DAY. THIS STOPS THEIR BODY FROM GETTING TOO USED TO ZERO GRAVITY AND HAVING PROBLEMS WHEN THEY COME BACK TO EARTH.

OUR CLOSEST NEIGHBOR

Mars is the most Earthlike planet in the solar system, and it wouldn't take years to travel there. Some scientists think humans could live on Mars if we terraformed it, or made it more Earthlike. A major part of terraforming would be making Mars's atmosphere able to heat the freezing planet.

Mars has minerals, such as iron, that could be mined and used for the construction of buildings. It also has ice that could be melted to provide water. However, in 2018, scientists realized terraforming the whole planet isn't possible.

MARS HAS ICE CAPS ON IT. IF THE PLANET COULD BE WARMED UP, THE ICE WOULD TURN TO WATER.

EXPLORE MORE!

PEOPLE HAVE THOUGHT FOR A LONG TIME ABOUT WAYS TO TERRAFORM MARS. NOTHING THEY'VE COME UP WITH SO FAR WOULD WORK. EVEN IF WE COULD CREATE A THICK, BREATHABLE ATMOSPHERE AROUND MARS, IT WOULDN'T STAY THERE FOR LONG.

Mars isn't quite inside the habitable zone, but it's not too far outside of it either. In fact, Mars is very similar to what Earth was like billions of years ago. When Earth first formed, it had no **oxygen**. Then **bacteria** grew, producing oxygen that slowly entered the atmosphere. This allowed larger plants and animals to grow.

Some people believe that bringing plants and other oxygen-creating creatures to another planet could help turn the atmosphere into something humans can breathe. The tricky part would be keeping the living things alive long enough for them to change the planet.

EXPLORE MORE!

IN 2019, TWO SCIENTISTS CAME UP WITH AN IDEA TO TERRAFORM ONLY PARTS OF MARS. THIS WOULD CREATE SMALL "ISLANDS" WHERE HUMANS WOULD BE ABLE TO LIVE. THEY PLAN TO TEST THEIR IDEA ON PARTS OF EARTH THAT ARE COLD AND DRY LIKE MARS, SUCH AS ANTARCTICA.

THESE ROCKS ARE CALLED STROMATOLITES. THEY'RE MADE UP OF SOME OF THE FIRST LIVING THINGS ON THE PLANET—THE BACTERIA THAT HELPED CREATE THE OXYGEN IN EARTH'S ATMOSPHERE.

EXOPLANETS

Mars is the best choice for a second home in our solar system, even though it can't be terraformed. However, scientists aren't limiting themselves just to our neighborhood. They're also looking at exoplanets, or planets outside the solar system.

As of 2023, scientists have found thousands of exoplanets. However, none of them are quite right for humans. They're too big or too small, too far from or close to their sun, have too much atmosphere or not enough, and many other problems. Some of these planets might be able to be terraformed many years from now.

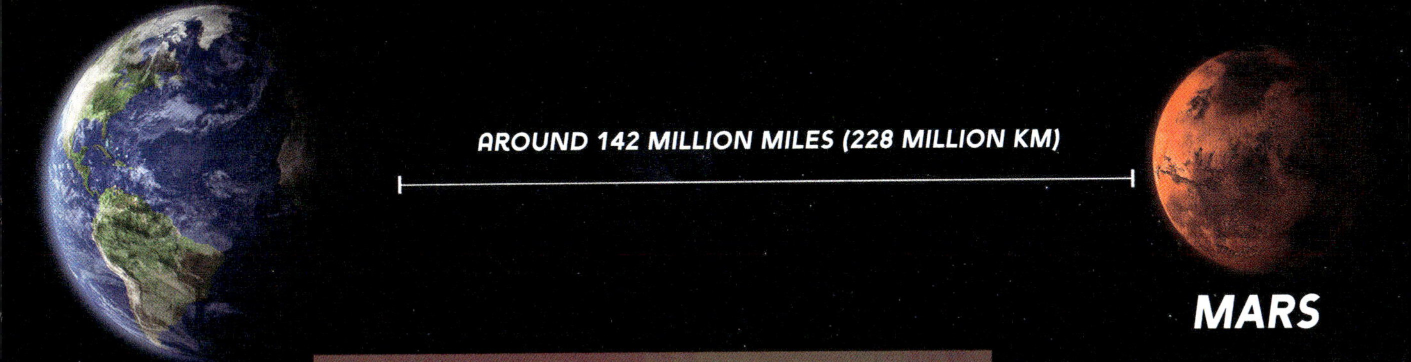

EXPLORE MORE!

MANY EXOPLANETS ARE SO FAR AWAY THAT IT WOULD BE IMPOSSIBLE FOR A PERSON TO REACH THEM IN THEIR LIFETIME. THIS IS PART OF THE REASON WHY PEOPLE ARE MORE INTERESTED IN LIVING ON MARS THAN ON ANY OTHER PLANET.

THIS PICTURE SHOWS ONE PERSON'S IDEA OF WHAT A TERRAFORMED PLANET MIGHT LOOK LIKE.

EARTHLIKE BUILDINGS

If we can't terraform a planet, people would have to find other ways to make it habitable. One idea is to put up special buildings on or below a planet's surface. They would have the air, water, and other materials needed to keep us alive.

Choosing the right planet would be important even with such buildings. The planet would have to have things people could use to grow food, fix buildings and machines, and make tools. This is because it would take too much time and money to keep sending things from Earth.

EXPLORE MORE!

THE HEALTH OF A PERSON'S MIND IS JUST AS IMPORTANT TO THEIR SURVIVAL AS THE HEALTH OF THEIR BODY. ANYONE LIVING ON ANOTHER PLANET WOULD NEED BOOKS, MOVIES, GAMES, OR OTHER THINGS TO DO FOR FUN.

BUILDINGS SUCH AS THESE MIGHT BE ABLE TO KEEP AN EARTHLIKE ATMOSPHERE INSIDE ON AN UNINHABITABLE PLANET.

A DIFFICULT TRIP

Right now, people don't have the ability to start living on other planets. Even getting to a planet as close as Mars would be very hard and costly. It would take a lot of **fuel** and a lot of time. It would also be dangerous, or unsafe, for the astronauts. If anything went wrong with the ship, there would be no way to help them.

Storing the large amounts of fuel, food, and oxygen people would need both before and after they land is another problem scientists haven't solved yet.

EXPLORE MORE!

AFTER A CERTAIN AMOUNT OF TIME SPENT IN SPACE, ASTRONAUTS START TO HAVE PROBLEMS WITH THEIR EYES. IF PEOPLE TRIED TO GET TO ANOTHER PLANET RIGHT NOW, THE LACK OF GRAVITY MIGHT CAUSE SERIOUS EYE ISSUES BEFORE AND AFTER ARRIVAL.

SPACESHIP FUEL TANK

IT TAKES A LOT OF FUEL TO GET A SPACESHIP OFF A PLANET. TO GET PEOPLE HOME FROM MARS, THE SHIP WOULD NEED TO CARRY ALL THAT FUEL WITH IT.

TIME TO GO

Some people wonder why we should bother looking for other habitable planets. One reason is that scientists believe the sun is getting hotter as it ages. In around a billion years, it will burn so hot that the oceans will boil away. Looking for a second home now could save people in the future.

Another reason people give is that humans are harming the Earth with pollution and using up many of its **resources**. However, many people say that instead of trying to leave Earth, we should do a better job of taking care of it.

SOME KINDS OF POLLUTION RELEASE GASES INTO THE ATMOSPHERE THAT TRAP MORE HEAT. THIS IS VERY BAD FOR LIVING THINGS, INCLUDING HUMANS. MANY PEOPLE ARE WORKING TO STOP THE PLANET FROM GETTING TOO HOT.

EXPLORE MORE!

ALL STARS DIE AT SOME POINT, AND OUR SUN WILL BE NO DIFFERENT. HOWEVER, IT ISN'T EXPECTED TO DIE FOR ANOTHER 5 BILLION YEARS. THE SUN'S INCREASE IN BRIGHTNESS IS NOT DIRECTLY CONNECTED TO ITS DEATH.

LIFE ON ANOTHER PLANET

What would it actually be like to live on another planet? A lot would depend on the kind of planet we find. If it's one with the right atmosphere, gravity, and liquid water, it will be easier than trying to make the planet habitable. However, there are some problems people will have to deal with no matter where they land.

One problem is the distance from Earth. Sending resources, messages, or people between the two planets could take months or years.

EXPLORE MORE!

PEOPLE MIGHT BE ABLE TO LIVE ON THE PLANET KEPLER-186F. IT'S ABOUT THE SIZE OF EARTH, AND IT'S IN ITS STAR'S HABITABLE ZONE. HOWEVER, IT WOULD TAKE MORE THAN 500 YEARS TO GET THERE, SO WE WON'T KNOW FOR SURE ANY TIME SOON.

MANY PEOPLE LIKE TO IMAGINE WHAT AN ALIEN PLANET WOULD LOOK LIKE. MAYBE IT WOULD HAVE TWO MOONS!

Another thing to think about is what's already on the planet. If we find a planet that has oxygen and liquid water, it's likely there's already some kind of life there. On Earth, we know which plants and animals are dangerous. On a strange planet, people would have to quickly learn which plants and animals to stay away from.

Right now, we're a long way from going to another planet. We might someday find one we can live on, but getting there will take many years. Until that time, it's fun to think about!

EXPLORE MORE!

SOME PEOPLE WANT TO GO TO OTHER PLANETS AND MOONS IN THE SOLAR SYSTEM TO DIG UP RESOURCES THAT COULD BE USED ON EARTH. INSTEAD OF MAKING THEIR HOME ON THESE OTHER WORLDS, PEOPLE WOULD ONLY BE THERE FOR A FEW YEARS TO WORK.

ANOTHER PLANET MIGHT HAVE GERMS HUMANS HAVE NEVER SEEN BEFORE. THIS MEANS IT MIGHT BE HARD FOR PEOPLE TO STAY HEALTHY ON THE NEW PLANET.

GLOSSARY

atmosphere: The thick layer of gases that surrounds the Earth or another planet.

bacteria: Tiny creatures that can only be seen with a microscope.

evolved: Changed little by little over a long period of time.

fuel: Something used to make energy, heat, or power.

gravity: The force that pulls objects toward the center of a planet or star.

joints: The parts of the body that bend.

muscle: One of the parts of the body that allow movement.

oxygen: A colorless, odorless gas that many animals, including people, need to breathe.

pressure: The application of force to something by something else in direct contact with it.

radiation: Waves of energy.

resources: Things that are found in nature and are valuable to humans.

solar system: The sun and all the space objects that orbit it, including the planets and their moons.

temperature: How hot or cold something is.

universe: Everything that exists.

FOR MORE INFORMATION

BOOKS

Hamilton, John. *Curiosity Rover: Searching for Life on Mars.* Minneapolis, MN: Abdo Publishing, 2018.

Leyssens, Jan. *Is There Life in Outer Space?* New York, NY: Clavis Publishing, 2021.

Williams, Dave, and Loredana Cunti. *Destination Space: Living on Other Planets.* Toronto, ON: Annick Press, 2018.

WEBSITES

BrainPOP: Mars
www.brainpop.com/science/freemovies/mars
Watch a movie, play games, and take quizzes to learn more about whether humans could live on Mars.

NASA SpacePlace
spaceplace.nasa.gov/all-about-exoplanets/en/
Read more about how scientists find exoplanets.

Space.com: "What Would It Be Like to Live on Alien Planet Kepler 186-f?"
www.space.com/29020-living-on-alien-planet-kepler-186f.html
Could this exoplanet be a second Earth? Read more about it here.

Publisher's note to educators and parents: Our editors have carefully reviewed these websites to ensure that they are suitable for students. Many websites change frequently, however, and we cannot guarantee that a site's future contents will continue to meet our high standards of quality and educational value. Be advised that students should be closely supervised whenever they access the internet.

INDEX